Prompts of the Heart

Prose and poetry

Dr. Manijeh Khorshidi

Cyberwit.net
HIG 45 Kaushambi Kunj, Kalindipuram
Allahabad - 211011 (U.P.) India
http://www.cyberwit.net
Tel: +(91) 9415091004
E-mail: info@cyberwit.net

Printed at VCORE.

To the loving memory of my father and mentor
who, through his love for God and His Manifestation
for this age, Baha'u'llah lived his life for the Oneness of humanity.

To my beloved mother, who was a true partner with
my father, and without her support and encouragement
I could not bring myself to write.

Contents

Be Our Custodian

Who would not love the serene, sheltering, and pleasing-to-the-eye trees with their dance-like movement, I thought to myself.

Trees are a reflection of the sacred in nature. They manifest life at its best. They are life-givers.

With all these attributes, no one has ever heard the voice of domination or boasting from them.

Every tree has its own tale. The day it was planted, the one who cared for it, and the time it started to come to fruition.

*The one who planted me,*the tree tells its admirer," taught me patience."

Growth was hard, the tree continues, *I had to endure a lot from the dirt, but my planter nurtured me to face the hardship of life.*

Then the tree becomes tall, independent, and strong. It does not need so much attention anymore.

It is time to give back.

It diffuses the love of the planter to the air indiscriminately through its leaves and branches.

The cycle of reciprocity starts. The gratitude of the tree even extends to mother earth as it returns its leaves to it.

What a bliss to be part of the whole!

Is the contribution of a small unpretentious tree not as valued as the mighty oak?

In the world of the trees, there is no discrimination. All are invited to participate in the feast of life. Reflection on the world of the trees reignites a glimpse of hope in my heart.

I do not have to be extraordinary to be a protagonist in the cycle of life, I thought to myself.

The loving gardener plants the seed of life and hope regardless of being able to reap the fruits of his effort.

With his insightful vision, he sees the hidden tree in the tiny seed.

Is it possible to extend this insight to the realm of education, and to see the gem-like potential embedded in every child?

The trees in my garden are inviting me to join them in praise and gratitude. *Be our custodian?* they say gently.

Winner of "Arbor Day writing contest" in Brookfield, WI, 2018.

Bride on Earth

The shimmering light of the sun
from winter blue sky
spread its rays on silent ground
enveloped with the snow cloth.

Like a peaceful bride
clothed in the white lacy gown
the snow-topped trees stand tall
with their fluffy branches and boughs.

The wounded land
now hidden under cover of snow
portrays a cosmic beauty
to the eye of the beholder.

The enchanted eye falls upon
the seductive scene.
The spellbound soul, the captivated heart
wonders at this bride on earth.

Ecstasy reveals itself
when we see the change in nature
the sign of growth, the moving cycle.
It entails the tale of love
the unseen-force driving life.

Cloud Rider

When I was growing up, I heard two phrases that my parents used quite often, and up to this day, the effect of these words has remained with me.

The first one, my father's favorite, was *'the next year.'*

The second one which strengthened the imagination was *'watch the clouds.'*

I heard this phrase mostly from my mother.

I realized later that these phrases and their application saved my parents from spending unnecessary expenses on their children.

My father taught science and mathematics in High school but being a philosopher at heart in every equation and phenomenon, he saw the mystery of life and its sacredness.

His students loved him for his ease of explanation of any subjects.

This ability to encourage the students and uplift their minds was one of his gifts.

He used this skill at home and practiced it with his children too.

With his teacher's salary, my father had to navigate keeping the balance between unreasonable and endless demands of his children and his income.

My mother, a true partner to my father, helped him raise an ark to sail the turbulent sea of their life.

I can still hear his gentle response wrapped with *'the next year'* to my every irrational want.

At the age of four, I wanted a pony, and a year later, I asked for two. Lack of logic in my demands encountered the futuristic and hopeful reply of *'you'll have it the next year,'* followed by *'God willing.'*

With having no clue of the concept of time, the next day or the next year meant the same to me. I could hear only the reassurance in his answer. And not knowing the meaning of *'God willing,'* I could only assume it was part of every sentence.

I found out later that reliance on God and exertion of efforts were wedded together and played as one force in my parent's life.

Life's moments bond together through the thread of love and hope in childhood. Thus, it makes the children the master of living.

The lingering question remains why do we leave these two qualities behind when we get to our adulthood?

The next year business never arrived, and my expectations never ended.

Being ever hopeful and waiting for a pony or other things kept me busy.

I never heard a negative response or disappointing reply from my father. His love and my hopes weaved together and formed patience in me.

My happy childhood did not entail possessing many toys and dolls, much less a pony. Besides, we lived in the city, and the yards in Tehran houses did not lend themselves to keeping any animals.

The demand for a pony which preceded by many others, followed only by even more.

None of them came to reality.

But I remember riding my pony many times. I see my four-year self playing in the yard with a few dolls and my imaginary pony captured from the clouds.

How easily children find forms and shapes in them, and how they let their imagination fly without any fear.

I found my pony and many other wishes in the clouds of the Tehran sky.

And that takes us to the second phrase which I constantly heard.

My mother taught her restless firstborn, to gaze at the clouds and find the things she wanted in them. This, I did and learned to be a cloud gazer fast.

Time passes, and I find myself on the other side of the world on long walks on the seashore in Northern Ireland.

Early November- cold makes its presence known to my body. When I left Tehran at the beginning of September, the pleasant air and abundance of flowers, and the language of nature did not convey cold weather. Also, lacking common sense, I packed one suitcase allowed to take with textbooks. But none of these books can keep me warm now in the chill of November in Northern Ireland, and I need a warm jacket. But I have to travel to another city to buy a winter coat.

The picturesque village where I live has a drug store and a Pup. Then, there is a post office. This place is the village hub. When you enter this small place, you see some cans of green beans and a few other grocery items. But more importantly, it operates as the Central Intelligence in the village. They are aware of any news or events.

When people are not in the pub, they are in the hub.

I never venture to the first one, but I start to frequent the latter.

I hear conversations such as:

Obrien has gone to Belfast today.

Mary Sullivan has her hand-made mitten and sweaters sale next week.

Donovan is getting married.

Murphy, and O'Leary, are going to business together.

A foreigner has moved to the village! Hay that is me!

This unknown territory to me becomes my new home. Forced transplantation brought me here. I find the gift of safety and abundance of care in this land. I had to leave Iran, the land of my ancestors who lived there for thousands of years. I had to leave my country where the systematic life-threatening conditions for the Baha'is, wealth seizing, and pillaging of their homes uprooted many such as my family.

Isolated in Northern Ireland and far from home, I find a familiar scene looking up.

I see the moving clouds in that quiet corner of the world.

Their inviting movements resemble the clouds in the Tehran sky. I am not four years old, and I do not look for a pony anymore. So why am I still attracted to the clouds?

Is it that the clouds are still capable of intriguing my imagination?

What can I get from this patchy white stuff?

I sit on a small rock and pull up my shawl, wrapping myself to stay warm. The sea has no objection to this wayfarer invading its solitude. And I look up. Then, suddenly I find myself flying on a falcon's wings, and before I know it, I am up in the air.

My voyage begins.

Looking down, I see the lands and the seas. I pass the mountains and the valleys. I can stop anywhere that I wish.

I wish to see my parents.

The roads appear one after another, and the doors get open.

Then I enter my parents' home.

I see Mom serving the Persian tea to their company and my father helping her. Their faces portray happiness. The living room looks ornate, just like the time in the past.

The soft breeze scatters the aroma of the running roses in the yard into the living room.

I hear the laughter of my father with his friend playing backgammon.

Why am I worried about them?

Nothing has changed! We are still together.

Then, I feel everyone's faces fade into the background.

I can't hear my parents' conversation anymore. They seem to be distant.

I blink, and I cannot find the falcon in the clouds.

I am back on the rock, thousands of miles away from my parents.

Immersed in sorrow, I find solace in my heart. My heart filled with joy I gaze up again and do not find anything this time in the clouds anymore.

Did my soul journey to a far-off land, leaving the time and space behind through the clouds?

Rumi comes to mind:

There is a life force within your soul, seek that life.

There is a gem in the mountain of your body, seek that mine.

Don't look outside, look inside yourself and seek that.

Wake up Lovers, It is time to start the Journey!

The ebbing sun casts its crimson light on the sea and turns the clouds into the burning bushes. Thus, nature writes another mystic tale of love and life with its mighty pen in the book of existence. It is time for me to return home. I

t dawns on me that no matter where our homes are and what land we dwell in, on every sunrise, we behold the clouds having a dance and the sea surging for us.

The theater of life and its opera belong to us.

Can we say then that gazing at the clouds without being in danger on the ground proves the claim of having a better world?

I catch myself following the clouds and riding on them quite often.

What a delight being childlike again, even for a few moments.

Hearing the news about the American hostages in American Embassy in Tehran creates another level of anxiety and worry.

A place where I had frequented the near places to it many times. The quiet neighborhood and tree-lined streets surrounding the Embassy also had the American Institute for learning English, where many Iranian students furthered their second language, including me.

Listening to the news means anxiety.

I hear from my father, who has stayed behind to support us less and less.

In the absence of his support, I have to find a way to sustain myself. I have no place to turn and no one to ask for help.

My life in Northern Ireland folds up after a while. I breathe its pure air with every breath and remain grateful forever to that land of lush green with its kind people.

In pursuing my livelihood, I follow the trail to London and make my home there. What will happen to me there?

Should I still look up and gaze at the clouds?

What do I find in the London sky?

Can I hope to find any falcon in the clouds to take me back home to see my father one more time?

Appeared on reedsy.com

Fascination with the Ancient Ruins

Oh, that mysterious power of ancient palaces and temples, even their ruins attract the soul and the heart of the beholder.

They remove the admirer from the domestic thoughts to the transcendence world of reflection and imagination.

Why this phenomenon?

Why this fascination?

Is it because these age-old temples and palaces enable us to gaze at our past, our frailties and hopes?

Is it because the past liberates us from the present?

Is it our mortality that incites us to bring the ghost of the past to life again?

And why do we want to retell their stories?

Whatever the reason, we are fascinated by the power of their silent stories.

One telling story is the tale of an ancient place in a far land.

Once upon a time, there was a King who built a beautiful Palace. Looking back we see a just king who loves his subjects, and whose palace stands as a testimony to the power and majesty of its royal resident.

Then it came the day when the painful fate of the palace changed everything.

Today the ruins of that Palace, naked from its glory still stands and possessed of pale majesty. Its remains can take the unexpected visitor to the sublime of praise and awe.

I am still here, I am still standing, a deep tired voice echoes in that ruined space. *I was the most magnificent one, I was called Persepolis.*

Any heart attuned to the echo in that space can hear the voice reminiscing.

Twenty-five hundred years ago, the King of Persia, Darius the Great, built me. He wanted me to be a masterpiece. Thus, I became one. A marvel of architecture in the world.

The Roman and the Greek envied me. One hundred twenty-five thousand square feet was my domain, not counting the surrounding hills and plains, over which I had spread my claim over them.

I was a gem-like, showpiece of symmetry and artisanship. The mountains behind me and the river at my feet were proud of my presence.

How vividly I remember the days of my glory," the tired voice of the ruined Palace continues.

The dignitaries from other regions came to see my stunning beauty. They came with the chariots, and stage carriages which were ornamented with gold.

I was built high on the hill, sixty-six feet above the ground. This allowed people to have a view of me from miles away. I was pleased with their adoration. I was built to be admired with no equal.

The visitor still hears the elated pride in the voice of Persepolis.

Can this untempered pride with untraceable modesty, be the arrogance of narcissism?

The independent self-glory?

That as well may be part of the fascination for Persepolis.

The mode of the aged voice changes to a felicitous tone and continues the ancient tale.

My King hosted his feasts and coronation here, the voice proclaims.

Those bygone days, the days when the grand hall was filled with flowers, ornaments, and scents.

The chosen musicians in the land played the songs of love in my halls. The beautiful maidens with long hair and colorful silk costume danced until dawn.

Those never-ending glorious days and nights of celebrating festivals of Sun, Harvest, and the New Year; how happy everyone seemed to be.

People came to offer their gifts of gratitude to the King whom they loved.

My walls and columns testify to the joy, to the energy of hope, and the richness of life in those days.

Until that fateful day, that dark, gloomy day, which changed everything.

The Voice becomes quiet, it almost disappears. As if it is the end of the story.

What happened? Tell me the rest, the captured beholder asks.

Moments later, a sigh gives hope to the expectant listener. The Voice continues, *the rumor was that my King had been killed in the battle with Alexander, miles away from Persepolis.*

It had to be true, as not long after, Alexander arrived in the Palace with all his army leaders. I could see the look of admiration on his young face.

The thirty-three year old conquerer loved my beauty. I heard him saying to his companion that he protects me from any harm. I could add to his prestige, to his fame, he said. I had made him "Alexander the Great." My fate was safe in his hand, or so I thought.

In honor of his victory over the greatest civilization, the Persian empire, the voice continues, *Alexander decided to have a majestic feast in his prized conquered Palace, a feast which was befitting me.*

He sacrificed to his gods.

Entertainment of all sorts, music, games, and abundant food were provided for the festivity.

The dark sky of Persia with its luminous stars gazed on me with grief that night. As if all the Heaven and Earth were aware of what was going to happen except me.

I was intoxicated by the admiration of the guests. Unaware of my imminent fate, I even forgot my grief of losing the King!!

The crowd was loud, they were drinking heavily.

Then, a seductive woman of Athenian origin whispered in Alexander's ear.

He was bewitched by this maiden. "Torch it" "Torch the Palace my great Alexander," she said.

Why did she want to set me on fire?

Alexander wanted to please her.

Thus, the torches of fire were gathered.

The drunken guests each possessed one with pride.

Musicians were playing for them but sounded the march of death to me.

Alexander and his mistress set the fire on me, followed by his accomplished army leaders and prominent guests with a procession of victory honoring their gods.

The orgy of my burning continued for hours.

Nobody dared to hear my lamentation, my painful cry that night, except the somber sky of Persia.

From the palace of beauty and grandeur, I became abandoned and burned-old palace.

The Conqueror carried away the treasures of Persepolis on the back of 20, 000 mules and 5000 camels.

That was the last time I saw Alexander. He ruined me and yet he wanted to own me. He could not, however, take my soul away. My story became pages of history.

The tired Voice goes away but leaves the beholder in a deep desire to imagine the living days of Persepolis.

Is that why these ancient ruines have remained so fascinating?

God-made Murals

Walking through the park, the oak tree with its fascinating fractal geometry summons me to itself.

For years, this tree with its long life lived and its epic tale of love and sacrifice has been a refuge for me.

The rain, wind, and nourishment from mother earth have sustained me. Giving back is part of the cycle of life. I hear the tree says.

In that space with its solitude, when I look at this tree, I hear the language of love and gratitude, of trust and reciprocity.

The forests, groves, and the valleys pride themselves to hear this language.

Anywhere they grow, they provide God-made murals.

Wherever they are, they sing the song of life. That ancient symphony, the divine melody, the magnum opera.

How often the dancing leaves of the tree have stimulated the poets to ink on paper their inspired intimation?

Kahlil Gibran believes: *Trees are poems the earth writes upon the sky.*

What is it about the trees, these mythical beings that we relate so much with them.

They have entered our consciousness. These silent teachers transcend the limits of forms.

Then, I hear the tree again:

I have always been true to my reality.

In many systems of beliefs and traditions the sacredness of life has been related to me.

Spiritual growth has been explained through me.

The great divine teachers have used me to teach the purpose of life through metaphors such as the tree of life, and the tree of knowledge.

If only we could pass this ancient wisdom to the future custodians of nature, our young children that

like the tree, they too can stay true to their reality.

They too can free themselves from the yoke of judgment and self-criticism.

They too can channel their energy for their emotional and spiritual growth.

For the well being of existence.

The chirping birds arrive to claim the tree for themselves.

Hay, I am still talking to the tree!!

I have to depart from my oak tree, the God-made mural and claim my afternoon tea.

Winner of Arbor Day Contest Brookfield, WI 2020

Grandfather's Tree

I find my grandfather sitting on a chair in the shady part of the backyard with closed eyes and a gentle smile on his face that betrays his calm.

A book half-opened rests on his chest, and glasses sit on top of his head. The almost five-year-old me gets closer and puts her head on his lap.

Without opening his eyes or uttering any words, I feel his gentle strokes on my hair. But I seek his attention and especially want his eyes to be open.

Is this a storybook Grandpa?　I whisper.

Grandfather smiles and opens his eyes. He removes the glasses and puts his book aside.

Knowing well that the pestering child does not allow him to rest or read. Then, gently, he takes my hand, and we walk toward the garden at the end of the yard.

He gets busy with doing gardening in the new section that he has created, and I see me running around and coming back to him as a touch base, as a safety point.

It is summertime, and Grandfather has come to visit and spend some time with us. In the evenings, I see him sitting with his pipe among the jasmine and rose bushes, under the apple tree with the last trace of sunlight slanting through them, taking a break from gardening. He often looks up the trees. It seems like he talks to the trees, hearing him reciting:

'Ye are the fruits of one tree and the leaves of one branch.'

Not understanding his view of the existence or even the words he utters, I am captivated only by him, neglecting all my dolls since his arrival.

The desire of this child to be around the aged grandfather with silky white hair is a mystery that we all might have experienced.

Is it the language of love that bonds these two separated generations?

Or is it the canopy of detachment in the last part of life that liberates the soul to enjoy the carefree attitude of the grandchild?

Whatever the reason, I felt safe and loved in my grandfather's orbit.

His reflective and poetic side was a fruit of his detachment. But his gift of making anybody the center of attention came from his entrepreneurship. And in that summer, I see myself to have his attention.

As his first grandchild, I am even allowed to touch his hair, to hold his pip!

I find myself dwelling around him.

My parents' faces are vague in my mind during those days. I see them in the distance, and my grandfather's illumined face gains distinction.

Then it comes the nights of Tehran. The cool fresh air, the star-filled sky become a lure to sleep outside. The gentle breeze going through the leaves makes them sing the song of timeless solace. Grandfather sits on a chair next to my bed with the mosquito net to tell me a story.

I enjoy listening to the tale with characters made up of the shape of stars.

He accompanies me to see a cluster of them that looks like the lion. Then he moves to the king with the crown, and even out of another group of stars, he guides my eyes to see the Simorgh bird of sovereignty. They all enter Grandpa's night stories.

The tired man has no respite, but my childish demands bring amusement to him.

If I only knew after that visit, I would never see him again?

The next day we venture out. He holds my hand, and we walk through the alley. He chooses the tree-lined road and looks at every tree with admiration. In crossing the street, he picks me up and puts me down on the other side. What a joy ride! We walk together again.

Where are we going? My feet are tired.

Sometime later, we reach the corner bakery. The aroma of fresh bread makes me hungry. I hear even the sound of fire, in the big oven built in the wall. I see one of the men put the long wooden shovel with the flattened dough into the fiery oven. Another man removes the baked bread and throws it on a stone to be picked up by the third person. They sing and repeat words with a rhythm. Other workers there take care of the customers. But those two perform on their theatrical scene with the oven at the center of their acts.

It is a scene to behold. The amused and pleased customers have no problem waiting. The place is too loud, and I hang tight to Grandfather.

We are on our way back home, and Grandfather has two pieces of fresh bread in his hand.

Tiredness has made me forget my hunger. I stop walking.

Then, I see him kneeling and helping me to climb on his back. My hands around his neck allow him to carry the fresh bread with one hand and hold my legs with another.

Later that day I see myself with my grandfather who plants a sapling in the backyard.

I bring water from the hose cup by cup, thinking I am helping him.

Why do you put your hands in dirt Grandpa? I ask.

'It is for you to enjoy the tree's fruits.' He says gently.

What fruit? I only see a few leaves on a twig.

My memory fails to remember more of that summer. Time passes. Grandfather lives in another city. Why does he not visit me anymore?

There is no clear answer. I hear he will come. But he never came.

Later I hear that Grandfather died after a short illness. His only request came to reality when he was buried under a tree. Sadness visits me. I long to be with him again. His short presence in my life stirs such deep emotions, which removes the time and space and puts me on his lap again in the garden that summer.

Sitting under the shade of the apple tree a decade later after Grandfather left us, I discern the meaning of the Sacred Words that a tender, wise man would repeat quite often whenever he would see a tree or plant it. It reveals his view of the world of existence.

The tree was a living example for him to see the unity of humanity.

He did not live to see the fruit of his labor as he died not long after planting the seeds and the young trees on that summer in our yard.

Every tree has a tale to tell. Recalling the gardener who with the hand of offering and affection planted them. Wherever on this earth, a tree grows, it sustains life, beauty and sings the anthem of reconciliation of the contraries with their universal tongue.

Remembering my grandfather, Rumi comes to mind:

On this earth,

In this soil,

In this pure field, let's not plant any seed
Other than seeds of compassion and love.

Years later, in a different land on another Continent, I find myself often retreating under the trees. The trees that other grandfathers have planted and possibly never lived to sit under their shade. Then, I hear the ode of praise of the tree. It echoes the space as its rustling leaves let the soft breeze waft through them.

On hearing this, my tired soul remembers my grandfather whose planted trees far away from me now shades others, and on praising the tree these words come to my heart :

Silence of your tongue inspires me
Your indiscriminating love embraces me.
Teach me O mighty tree
The mystic rhythm of life
That ancient wisdom of yours

Maybe that is one of the reasons we, the mortals, plant the trees to be our solace and console. The mystical syntax of nature encourages the soul to read the poetry written in the Manga Carta of creation, nature, which reveals the code of love and life. Whenever I look at a tree I see the face of my aged grandfather who out of his love for humanity wherever he went, planted seeds and seedlings. He offered affection to his surroundings like all other gardeners and sprinkled the spirit of sacrifice to the world.

I continue to look up like my grandfather to every tree and perceive the unity he saw in creation. And those Sacred Words that he would recite often reveal their meaning to me.

I miss my grandfather and the trees he planted in a far-off land.

I Am Here to Help

The call of the first lonely tree in ancient times has been the same as the trees in the forests and on the slopes of mountains today, *'I am here to help.'*

And ever since, they are into a covenant with mother nature.

They observe the law of creation and are proud to be part of this magnificent structure in the universe. They provide help without expecting to be acknowledged.

Yes, trees are essential to enrich the soil, purify the air, provide oxygen, balance the ecosystem, and prevent floods.

But there is a myth and magic about them, intriguing the soul to soar to celestial realms and evoking the imagination to depict them on paper.

What is their tale?

How could they be a source of joy and empowerment?

Trees humbly offer a loving consolation through show not tell, a transcendent way of comforting.

I hear the tall tree gently tells this inconsolable soul, *'I am the same tree in your native land where under the dark sky of the East you would sleep with my quiet song.'*

'You can hear the same song far from time and space in the past,' the tree continues.

'Here or there, wherever you are, life is within you.' *'Here or there, you can give back and spread your roots.'*

Is it the accent of their language that grants them myth?

The language of ever-present love and upliftment to the heart?

Then, eyes fall upon the shrubs and saplings growing under the mighty oak. How beautifully the harmony of this inter-generational coexistence has survived in nature.

Even in death, the trees preserve their sacredness. The poet's grief leading to his masterpiece comes to mind, a requiem revealing the circles of life in the book of creation as another masterpiece.

In life and death, they give.

The sound of mother earth echoing in the air proclaims how proud she is to take the fallen trees back to her bosom.

The tale of trees is long, and their myth cannot be exhausted. But the protective canopy of trees remains constant in our lives.

Winner of Arbor Day Contest in Brookfield, WI 2021

Journey on Earth

The swift journey on earth entails joy and pain,
we till the soil, build monuments years later leave it behind.

Others come along to find the field plow the earth,
then it comes to their turn to take their flight.

To wrap up the tale, we arrive and leave,
never mind being attached to this world of dust.

We never had the right to own this passage,
the claim remains to care for and pass it on.

 The bird of soul ever free from the burden of soil
 destined to wing its flight to that space beyond on high.

Like a drop happy to merge with Ocean of Life,
radiating like the ray from the blazing Sun.

The limits of this life will pass, I tell myself.
Happy the soul perceives that Ocean, that Sun.

Dedicated to Iranian women whose cry for equality has emerged since 1844 by Tahirah Qurrat Al-'Ayn, the Pure One (1818-1852)

Let Me live

An ancient cry calls from a distance
The cry of Let Me Live
a quiet cry from the heart with no word or sound
a cry never acknowledged, never heeded
a cry ever-faded to insignificance, to pages of oblivion
with no face appearing with the cry
the faceless lament ignored for centuries
in Iran, a fallen land from its ancient glory.

With the passing of time, the quantum breeze
transmits the silent cry in the womb of time.
The age-old cry of Let Me Live
begins to find a form, a face.
The nascent call soars fast.
The sudden call from the clarion of the divine,
carries a sound never been heard before
the cry that has a sword
the sword of sounds, syntax, and words.
The song of salvation, liberation, and the right to be
reverberates in mountains, valleys, the earth, and heaven.

It is the mid-nineteen century
the awe-stuck beholders see the figure of a woman
who speaks, utters, and confronts.
There it is, the Poetess!

Being called Tahirah, The Pure One, the Solace of the eye!
Standing in the middle of a plain
on the slopes of a mountain
with creeks going through and surrounded by trees.
The veilless Poetess addresses the assemblage of men with the
knowledge of old and new.
The eye of time had never seen such a creature.
She says women and men are equal. Strange!
She says women and men are the two wings of the bird of
humanity.
She says the wings are equal but different.
*Then, she utters the final words you can suffocate me, but
you can't prevent women's liberation.*
Every one believes
She is mad!
For sure has lost her mind!

The curses and blasphemy verbalize the violent voices of men.
She cannot be a woman if she talks, the assemblage cries!
She cannot be a woman if her face is exposed!
Purity has vanished in her.
The honor has evaded her.
Where is the man in charge of her?
Where is the cover to clothe her? to make her unseeable again?
Bewildered scholars, the furious knowers, do not know anymore.
They scream the world has come to an end.
Some escape the gathering on that day a few cut their throats to
show their deploration of her.

A prodigy as a child, a philosopher of life, a believer in justice,
a fresh air for the choked women
an aspiration and hope for all the helpless ones
with all her gifts, the Poetess remains

a regret to her father for not being the son.
The fire of love for divine Beloved
has burned attachment to her lower self.
Thus, she is selfless, enlightened, and has discernment.
A celestial deluge flows from her heart.
The gem-like words reveal from her tongue.
The ink of her passion baffles the pen of knowledge.

The question remains for men in that land
how to face the New Message the Poetess believes
'Equality of Genders' is the most perilous word of all
to turn to it or deny it.
To see her as a human with rights or a forgotten one with crimes
the fury boils in their hearts.
what becomes of them if they accept the new Words
they will lose their power over women,
the ones supposed ever fading on the canvas of life
the ones supposed to be hushed in the passage of time.
The call has trembled the hearts of the fearful
the ones with names and fame
the ones with possessions, the seats of honor.

The verdict arrives:
this woman cannot lower our rank
nor can she change our ordered lives!
Remove her, destroy her.
She misleads women to open their cages.
Eradicate her.
The Will of God is this, religious leaders say.
The veil of self has blinded them to Truth
the weight of ego descended them to gloom
howling curses on the Poetess
the leader's signature carries with force to put her to death.

The tale that began on that summer day
at the verdant plain named Badasht in Iran
has remained in the tablet of time
carved in crimson letters
written on the chests of seekers of Truth.
The Truth that has vibrated the atoms and unlocked the gate of hearts.
The universe has heard the lament of centuries of sorrow
an epic tale of pain.
The handmaiden chained to the past
releases herself at last.
The Poetess sings the song of time to come
a prototype for women to wing their flight
to soar high in the fathomless sky
singing the song Let Me be Myself.

The rejoiced souls, emancipated from the past
the followers of Light, the believers in Truth
the ones who heard the Pure One
with courage give their lives
for freedom of thought, belief, and life
with hearts removed from freight
they see the Sun and abhor the bats of night.

The treader of an uncharted path
the sprinkler of love on flakes of hope
the One who has chanted the melody of emancipation of women
all her life
the One who did cleft asunder the veils of blindness
the One who removed the chains of thralldom
and in the final act in that Plain on that summer day in August
removed the cover from her face to bring life to the hearts of
some and terrorize others' hearts
is being captured and imprisoned by those fearful men.
The symphony of Poetess' life closes to an end.

A dark well, far and out of town at the time
becomes the abode of the lifeless body of the Brave One.

The women, the descendants of the Pure One
in the land of Iran today
the young and aware of their reality
wanting their destiny in their own hands
those with conscious, with faith in humanity
serenading the song of 'Women, Life, Freedom.'
Since that eventful day in 1844 in that unknown Plain
a path appeared for women to walk
a space to move forward, to find their calling
a trail colored by the crimson blood of thousands of women and men
who turned to the New Sun in the sky of beliefs
who heard the Poetess as one true believer in the New Message.
 A most mystical tale of love that remains in the heart of the universe.

An ancient cry calls from a distance
To some, the cry of Let Me Live
remains still a transgression
Many are in doubt as ever.
They repeat the tainted message of the former time to women.
Where to go, you little creature?
Misery comes to you with your flight
The chain on your feet is bright and golden!
The shackle brings you protection!

A flood of unwritten letters, those unplayed notes
has permeated the domain of consciousness
Those who heard the handmaidens
released themselves from heedlessness.
The voice of the wronged-ones
echoes the space of immensity.

The free-ones in ascending utters
Nevermind shielding us
The golden cage is yours. Preserve it.
Emancipation will be ours to cherish it.

An ancient cry calls from a distance
O thou Pure One, O Tahirah
how your words transformed the hearts
the beauty of your face remains with us in life
your sacrificed life, a ransom for the redemption
of all who bravely step in the path of justice
of those who chant
Women, Life, Freedom
Let Me Be Myself
Let Me Live.

"Regard Man as a Mine Rich in Gems of Inestimable Value."

My father, as a teacher, lived by this powerful and profound quote from the Baha'u'llah. His students flourished under this embracing and inclusive method of teaching.

But it took me years to understand the true meaning of these words and the reason behind my father's attachment to them.

His philosophy in teaching carried no authority over the students but empowered them.

I witnessed this one day in ninth grade when I sat in one of his classes. My school is closed on that day. My father encourages me to go to his school to see if I approve of his teaching.

He is proud of his daughter, I think to myself.

That is why he wants to show his student how a good student should look.

I am sure that he wants them to know how they should study more just like me and not to waste their time?

All these egotistical assumptions lure me against my reluctance to give consent, and so I go.

The second I arrive in his crowded classroom in that public school, I regret it.

There is not even a place for me to sit. One of the students moves a little bit, and I sit on the edge of the chair.

I feel at unease to be there.

First, because I am the teacher's daughter and all the eyes fall on me. But soon, fortunately, that disappears, and they release me from their surveying eyes. Indeed when I take time to look at them, they seem to be accepting and kind. What a relief!

Then the horror engulfs me. Mortified with the way my father handling his seemingly chaotic classroom, I recoil to an uncomfortable space in my mind. A place called embarrassment.

His classroom does not resemble any of my classrooms. With no visible order, I see only chaos in motion.

I ask myself what kind of teacher my father is?

He seems so powerless and subdued by his students.

Where is his authority?

Why doesn't he show his commanding power as a teacher?

My teachers silence us as soon as they enter the classroom. We, the students, feel their thunderous dominance, witness their power, and fear them. And in that atmosphere, we try to learn. In the name of order and structure, we never become protagonists in our learning.

I witness that every student participates in discussion, all have a voice. Every appropriate comment meets the praise of my father. The inaccurate ones find their place in the light of their intended meaning. All of a sudden, the classroom becomes a safe space for discovering your capacities. Teaching takes a new shape, and learning arrives joyfully in the lives of the students.

I see that the students love to be there. Their energy and happiness amaze me, as I have never witnessed with the students in my classes.

Later I learn that they ditch their classes to come to my father's classes. No wonder there is no place to sit.

I hear him putting questions to the students to reflect on. He assures the students that there is an insight in any answer, inviting everyone to participate in the discussion.

He reminds them to be resilient in thinking. I hear him emphasizing that the process of learning is more important than memorizing the textbook.

How about if we look at it this way? He says.

Can we consider it in any other way?

I hear things that I never heard from teachers in my private school.

Puzzled by his tolerance and open-mindedness, I am shocked to observe the deep affection and respect of the students towards him.

How can that be? My teenage brain cannot grasp the tenderness of teaching.

But here, in this classroom, a different narrative of education emerges.

Its invisible order prevails.

Later that day, I hear my father saying: 'Every student has something to contribute even if he not being aware of it,' He believed in the *'mine rich in gems.'*

These days, with passing decades from that day in my father's school, this quote opens a world of hope and light for me.

Whenever I meditate on these words, their twofold meanings touch my heart.

First, it releases me from the fear of inadequacy.

Then it takes me to a place where I look at everyone around, anyone that I know and do not know, as having capacities and capabilities which manifest themselves through nurturing and care.

These days, I realize that my seemly powerless father in his classroom was a master teacher and a master miner.

That was what he did.

He considered himself as one of the miners in the lives of those youth.

He purposefully engaged himself in exposing and mining the hidden gems in his students.

His unconventional method of teaching rendered the best result year after year.

In any class he taught, students had the highest rate of passing grades. They became such mines discovered and tapped with nurturing encouragement.

The most significant discovery in our lives is when we unearth our reality. And when we realize our unlimited gifts and capacities.

I miss my father and his gentle yet powerful way of life.

I miss his mentorship and the accompaniment which he provided in every stage of my life.

How beautifully he taught me to be resilient and not judgmental.

How ignorant I was that day in his classroom judging him for not knowing his craft of teaching.

How little I knew

The moment I judged you.

How mystifying

The moment I knew you.

To not relapse and forget that there are valuable gems in each of us, I have put a framed copy of these words in my study.

I know that if I ever disregard the essence and meaning of these words of wisdom, I might become the ninth-grader again with an ego that sees control as a way of order.

Not knowing that forced imposition does not uplift the soul.

It does not inspire the heart.

Then there is no learning involved, and life without the yearning to learn is a blank board with no letter on it.

How spectacular the day is when the gems of our being unveil themselves. The gifts which bring prosperity to ourselves and others.

Seven Valleys

They carry me to a house with a marble floor and high ceiling. The place is on the slopes of Mount Damavand in the north of Tehran.

The sadness of leaving my friends behind changes into a joyful feeling when I arrive in that spacious place.

There are plenty of beautiful objects and decorative pieces around. They are all in harmony with my beauty.

I met my new owner for the first time when he stepped into the art gallery.

He passed by me, then he returned and gazed at me with praise. Then he held me, and at some point, even caressed me!

I felt his adoration and was elated.

Many had praised and coveted to own me. But this master's look was different. He did not just admire and pass by me.

He adored, lingered, and claimed me.

It is a few years that I call that place home.

I am one of my master's most precious Persian carpets.

My master has hung me on the wall between his two cherry wood bookcases. He studies for hours in this favorite room of his. Sometimes his lovely young wife joins him.

They talk about the books they have read and poems they have written.

I hear them talk about the Seven Valleys of spiritual life.

The first Valley is **the Valley of Search**, he says. Search for Truth, that ultimate Reality.

Then looking lovingly to his wife, he adds that **the second Valley is Love**.

I listen to their intoning with the words of God.

Their inner joy uplifts the space.

Their reverence for nature and the divine extends to arts.

I cannot wait to hear the rest of the Valleys. But, it is mid-morning, and they have to leave.

The aroma of the fresh flowers in the ornamented vase has filled the room.

By their admiring look at me, it is as if I am part of their morning conversation.

"Life is good," I tell my silky body.

Recently, though, in their silent moments, they look out of the window and sigh.

I am puzzled. Why this momentary sadness?

Why the pausing sorrow?

I have never been in an atmosphere like this home. I have never been to anyplace like this.

They own me, but they do not covet ownership of me.

They have me, but they never inflate their ego with possessing me.

For the first time, I perceive myself through listening to these two love birds.

I hear them talking about service to humanity.

I see them meditating every day and reflecting on detachment.

And then, I learn from them that the purpose of every object is to serve others. To elate and to inspire the soul.

Thus, my purpose as a beautiful object is to bring joy to the heart of the beholders. And not to be attached to my beauty.

I never knew that. I have always been treated and looked at differently.

My story began centuries ago. Once upon a time, an elder artisan master took it upon himself to create his best work. It took him and his workers more than two years to make me.

They used silk and natural colors with shades of turquoise and ash-rose in my making.

When finally I came out of the workshop, I became the masterpiece and the last work of the famed artisan.

The account of my availability reached the ears of art hunters.

The walls of palaces and mansions became my home. Whoever had more power or wealth owned me.

I have tales to tell of my long journey during the last two centuries.

I lived as a neglected but a showpiece at best places until that day in the gallery when my new master purchased me and gave me a position of ornamentation and inspiration in his household.

He and his wife saw in me the artisanship, the creativity of craftsmanship.

They saw in me the labor and care of the young women of the past, those whose slender fingers made me.

They saw my actuality. I was honored and discovered for the first time.

Reminiscing on my life while I am in the serene space of my master's house gives me a perspective on ownership.

I compare my past owners who owned me with greed and my master's ownership who owns me with pride. Not pride of having me, but of my coming to being.

Oh, how much I want him and his family to be my companion forever. Sometimes you want to forget part of your life, the time of consternation and subjugation. I want to forget the period between my artisan maker and my new master, the one who made me with his gift of creativity. And the one who owns me with his gift of discernment. Feeling empowered and not overpowered, I throw a pleasing glance on my body and admiring look at my environment.

At the beginning of the Autumn, the silent moments of my master become longer.

His eyes betray a deep concern which I do not perceive the reason.

He is, as usual, gentle and generous. His calm removes anxiety, and his manner reassures everyone. Thus, the servants and helps who love their employer have no distress working there.

But the disquieting look in my master's eye worries me.

They still come to their library every morning and meditate. My master's wife still brings fresh flowers early morning to the room before their morning studying.

At one time, I hear her quietly reading to her beloved husband:

What if we lose everything,

What if the imperceptive slay us?

Rose is the rose in the garden or the vase

The soul is free, dwelling in the body or above.

What if we become dust on the ground?

Isn't this world shadow of the next?

Isn't death take us to the Valley of Light?

Then, the unthinkable happened.

And I discovered the cause for my master's concerns a few weeks ago.

At midnight on a cold night of Autumn, somebody pounds on the door. The servant runs and opens it. A friend of the family with a disheveled look appears at the door. He lets himself in and calls for my master.

'What is going on,' my master asks him while he puts on his robe, coming down the steps.

'They are looking for you,' the man says,' they are only two blocks away. 'You must leave immediately.'

The next thing I see is my master with his wife leaving the house hurriedly.

Their last gentle glance falls upon me.

Then silence fills the house.

Lonely and in the dark, I stand there as a witness.

It does not take that long that some angry men attack the house. They seem to be like crazed animals. They pillage, break, and burn.

Their first aim is the library. Why?

"Destroy those forbidden books," an angry voice filled with hate orders. 'Burn the books,' the man commands.

I am terrified. I feel the blaze of fire is catching up with me. For years I have been the companion of these precious books. They contain beautiful words of wisdom, divine philosophy, and history, especially the book of Seven Valleys which by now I have memorized.

But now, one by one, they become ashes.

Suddenly, a hand with a harsh movement pulls me down, rolls me, and puts me on his shoulder.

Where am I going?

Why this act of savagery?

And what happened to my master and his wife?

It is chaos in the city. The targeted homes are all on fire, homes with the book of Seven Valleys.

Now, it is many years that I am rolled up and put in the corner of this dark storage house. Once in a while, a man with a turban comes to check on me. With no shame in his unlawful possession, he admires me. I am his most prized take from the pillage that night. The man has possessed other beautiful objects from the house of my master too. We all lament together, remembering the calm and beauty of the space where our master so gently took care of us.

The depressive days of my life in this dusty place pass with the grieving of being far from my true self. I have become a commodity again. The possession of greed and wants. My values have become the material one only. The language of love and creativity weaved into my being, forgotten. Rolled up and limited, cornered and closed-lip, I only harbor hope of liberation.

One day the turbaned man brings another person to the storage room. They talk for a long time and haggle over the price on me. The unscrupulous keeper of me wants to make the most money of his unlawful take. Eventually, he sells me for an exorbitant price. I become the possession of a new owner, and I see the light of day at last.

Not knowing where he is taking me, I am happy to be owned by a man who lawfully purchased me.

He carries me to an art gallery.

He owns the place, and with the utmost care, opens me to praise his deal. He looks for a prime location in his shop to expose me to art lovers.

I am hung on the wall again.

Years pass, and I am in exposition. Then it comes a day when an adoring beholder arrives in the gallery. He moves close to me. I perceive a deep connection with this patron.

He is not as young as my master, but his look and charm are like him.

He lingers and adores.

He touches me gently with admiration. Could he be my own master?

I have become myself again and liberated. These days the room I am part of the decoration is the library in another beautiful house.

My new owner received me from his father as a gift for their wedding.

His father purchased me on that day from the gallery.

Ever since the question, of whether he was my original kind owner or not has stayed with me.

This young couple loves to offer hospitality to their friends and family.

One evening when they had a gathering, I heard their conversation on **the Seven Valleys.**

What is this? I thought to myself.

Why is it that when I hear the spiritual words, I feel like myself?

Their discussion reaches **the Valley of Contentment.**

Then, I see the man who purchased me from the gallery sitting in the corner quietly. His silver hair and wrinkles have made him look older than his age.

His son tells the story of his parents for the friends in the room.

He tells the story of the attack on his parents' property and how his father, by accident many years later, found his favorite Persian carpet stolen from him years before.

He tells the audience that this carpet was a gift to his mother by his father on their wedding day. And now he has gifted him and his wife with the same carpet.

He looks at his gentle father. His tearful eyes and smile tell the story of a life with pain and joy.

Then, after all, it was my master who rediscovered me at the gallery. My delight has no limits.

But I do not see the lovely wife of my old master in the crowd. The one whom every morning would bring fresh flowers to the library. Where is she?

What happened to her?

Looking at my old master, it is as if he remembers his wife's poem:

What if we become dust on the ground?

Then, I hear the son telling the rest of the story that his mother died when he was five, prematurely and unexpectedly.

She passed away with complete surrendering to the end of this first life, with her soul in contentment soaring to the realm of eternity.

I suddenly remember that **the Valley of Contentment** is another stage of the Seven Valleys.

Oh, I know I will be happy in this place, the house of master's son. I am beside myself that they hung me on the wall in the library filled with books about love and life.

Solomon of Love

Solomon of love quests for Sheba,
longing for the breeze from Eden of the East.
Discerning the sweet wafting wind, that everlasting scent,
that brings a dance of love carries hope and light.

Day and night, with fire at heart,
the king's hands open up to heaven to pray
with forehead low on the ground to praise.
At all times,
the beauty of Beloved, the Queen of Sheba, he remembers well.

The pain of separation the impatience present as ever,
reunion eludes the King of love.
Land of Beloved is so close, yet so far,
patience has ever been the steed of the search.

Soon arrives, the nightingale,
a harbinger of glad-tiding.
The Beloved is near, is near, it says.
Open your eyes, O Solomon, and trace the scent of love.

The Solomon of love takes the scented Path,
a scene to behold, the search for Truth.
The unfading Splendor is near.
The transcendence is in reunion
with true Beloved.

The tale of life may become as such:
Discern with heart, nevermind mind.

Never let the cold dwell at heart.
Let it be a place for the Love of God.
Let us all search for Spiritual Sheba.
Let us all be the Solomon of love.

The Crimson Leaf

On an autumn day, cool and brisk
falls on the ground, a crimson leaf.
Quiet, serene, with an elegant tongue,
tells a tale of its short-lived life.

The Passer-by beholds in awe
the red leaf and its end of life.
Sober of the past, surrendered to now,
leaf dances with the drifting wind.

Painter draws the leaf on canvas.
Poet puts it on paper.
Mystic retains this rhapsody at heart.
But the child plays with fallen leaves.

The color, form, and movement,
all become part of the child.
He cherishes being with leaves,
to feel and immerse in nature.

So modest but immense it is
the offering of a fallen leaf to us.
To perceive other gifts in life,
let us be a child at heart.

Removing the gathered dust
from the mirror of the heart,
allows us to absorb meanings,
let us embrace whole beings.

With a glowing face in submission,
the crimson leaf is trodden on.
Never seen again by the passer-by.
Ever remains in the cycle of life.

The Forgotten Ones

It is a day, like any other day, in a rural area in Iran.

We see the faces of two strangers whom we might know by heart.

They stand next to each other in their simple village attire.

They are farmers.

Their sun-trenched faces betray their hard life on the small farm they own. Their unassuming yet staunch figures show exuberant joy.

A moment of life is captured from them in a black and white photo a few weeks before the last scene of their lives is set in motion.

It is said that their loving and helpful attitude in life kept them happy despite all the difficulties the Islamic government heaped upon them. Foes and friends testified to their moral courage.

With no fame or wealth, they sprinkled generosity on all.

With no name or trace, they lived with transcendence.

With no indulgence or sense of superiority, they vibrated every atom of earth they trod.

Moth-like, they followed the light of goodness. And they had become a magnet for luminosity.

But they do not fit the everyday heroes we read about in the books.

No word is written about them, much less a book.

How does a soul desire to be in the orbit of these modest people? To dwell in their precincts and absorb their blazing love.

It seems that their simple life went on until that fateful day.

The day when like any other day, they rose to start their tasks on the farm and fed their few live stocks.

And the story begins:

They hear the loud sound of an angry mob coming toward their house.

Who are they? The wife asks

What do they want?

A sudden sense of grave danger takes over them, and they recall previous attacks on their live stocks and farm by fanatic Muslims.

But this time, they see more people all having stones or hatchets in hand.

Before they know it, the mobs attack their abode. They take the husband while beating him to the barn.

The world watches through the eyes of neighbors who pull down the curtains. Those who close the windows and let the darkness prevails.

Thus, the courage falls on mother earth's lap to witness the crime.

The attackers have an orgy of savagery. They pour gasoline on the severed farmer and set him on fire.

On that day, the cry of the farmer burning alive was only heard by the consciousness of humanity. Those who had the capacity to behold the face of love in the mirror of their hearts.

Far and distant, the question in the womb of earth is: are they done?

No, of course not. The mobs shouting the name of their god venture after the wife, whom they already have battered and kept in the house.

The smoke and fire from the barn convey the worst syntax of cruelty and give an impetus to the beaten wife to release herself to be with her husband. With her last trace of life, she runs out only to find a heap of dirt and ruins.

The next scene takes us to where we see the wife kneeling next to the charcoal remains of her husband. Between the ashes and smoke, she becomes the prey again.

But this time, she is not worried about her husband. They cannot do any more harm to him!

She remains without any resistance to the beating.

A few minutes later, her hacked body lay beside the remnants of her husband.

Abandoned until the dark of the night with no one to collect their remains, their tales remain with the earth.

The mobs have finished their task of being inhuman.

Lives taken. The story ends.

Next, we see the attackers leave the village.

The bats of night, hating the light and in hunt of more innocent Baha'is somewhere else, move on.

Their thirst for blood has subsided for a while, however. And other innocents can live their numbered days.

It is the heart's intelligence that remembers the two farmers. And then, the words begin to appear, a symphony starts to shape, and a poem comes into existence.

On that day, the world's eye witnessed the human flesh firework. The characters in this drama never lost their reality and did not linger to be rewarded for their good deeds.

If there is a domain where these forgotten ones dwell, we can discern a landscape ornamented with the ocean of forgiveness, forests of mercy, and many moons of generosity.

A place where the soul thrives, and pain and suffering do not exist.

Their unrecognized sainthood and unacknowledged heroism are only penned in unpublished books and read by those illiterate in hatred and darkness.

Yes, it is a day like any other day, with the sun rising and trees shading the earth, except the lament of the burdened ground from the blood of the innocents everywhere echoes higher and higher in the world of being.

The Humble Sword

People stand in line to look at an unassuming piece of steel in the Archives Building in Haifa, Israel.

The reverence and love of pilgrims approaching the relic are evident.

The sharp blade, the curvature of its body, and its polished metallic reflection are pleasing to the onlookers.

But, there is nothing special about this object at first glance. It is just a *Sword*.

Some of the visitors have seen worldly swords.

Could it look like one of the famous swords from the Middle Ages?

Undoubtedly, it is not El Cid's, the one he used to fight the Moors in the tenth century. That one is a cherished relic kept in Spain.

It is not Napoleon's as that is a national treasure in France, nor is the Scottish Knight of the twelve century that is kept in the Museum of Scottland.

Then, where does this sword come from?

Why do people from thousands of miles away come to have a glance at this sword?

The language of this sword is mythical, yet simple like its appearance.

If we listen in the silence of our souls, we can hear its voice uttering these words:

I have come from a distant land.

The hands of an old artisan, who loved justice more than anything else, made me.

He was a skilled craftsman who suffered death at the hand of the cruel King.

No hand touched my body with kindness anymore. Thus, I was abandoned in my maker's workshop to gather dust for many years.

Then came the day when a gentle hand picked me up and talked to me.

I wish not to shed the blood of innocents, he said.

Help me then to defend the defenseless, he added.

I had a mission now, and that brought me joy. It was 1848 in Iran.

My simple shape had not deterred my new master from caring for me.

Suddenly, and to my disappointment, I realized My master's right hand had a tremor!

How could he be a swordsman?

How could he use me with such a weak hand?

I wanted to show him my ability despite my lack of ornamentation. I indeed had no enameled handle or jeweled sheath, but my maker had made me solid. I wanted to show how sharp and effective I could be.

I wanted to be in a solid hand, not his hand.

Disappointed and ashamed, I felt more comfortable remaining in my sheath and hidden from the eyes.

The sword continues its story:

Time passed, and my master took me to different parts of the land, always sheathed.

I was beginning to believe that he would never use me. After all, he was a man of God.

Then came the day when my master was besieged with other men like himself in a fortress near the Caspian Sea.*

What was their crime?

It was the cry of justice and renewal that they had raised in a land of injustice.

Thus, the King sent his army of thousands of trained soldiers and heavy artillery against three hundred and thirteen men, some of whom had not even used a sword.

Who was their leader?

My young master, the one with the trembling hand!! The one who had never used me.

The King's army assumed that they could devastate and uproot the besieged men in amatter of a few hours, at most one or two days.

Hence, the attack started, and my master despite his contempt for taking lives, drew me with such might and vigor that, for a moment, I thought I was in the hand of a mighty warrior.

What is going on? I wondered. My master used me with such power that frightened the opposing army.

I have to say at all the confrontations, the army of the King was defeated by this small group of untrained defenders.

The soldiers could not understand why.

They came to believe that I had an unusual power — this brought terror to their hearts. But I knew the power was in my master's trembling hand!

He wanted justice, and I had become the instrument of that justice.

The few hours became seven months, yet the army could not defeat these lion-hearted men.

At last, the King had to devise a deception in order to defeat my master and his fellow warriors.

He sent his prince to convince these surrounded men to put their swords down in the name of their Holy Book, Quran.

There came the end of the defeder's lives. They were lured out of the Castle by the deceit of the government.

As soon as they put their arms down, they were all slaughtered, except a few who managed to escape in the dark of the night.

They lived to tell this tale of courage and betrayal.

I take pride remembering this episode of my life, the sword says, *as I never shed the blood of innocents.*

Visitors and pilgrims still travel to Haifa to see this Sword** and hear its tale.

* Fortress of Tabarsi is located on the way to the Caspian Sea in the north of Iran. It witnessed one of the shameful slaughters of the defenders of human rights, freedom of thoughts and religion.

*The sword belonged to Mulla Husayn, the first Letter of the Living. Refer to Nobil's Narrative for more details.

The Map of the Other World

Where can one find the map?
The map of the other world?
The world of meaning, that spiritual path?
If there is none,
why bother to get lost?
The searching soul asks.

Silence canopies the air.
The Wise man utters then:
No need to tread the market to unearth a map.
The seeker's desire
the guide to the other Path
abides within thy own self.

The pilgrim on this road,
the Wise man voices:
perceives the scented trail.
But first, thou must cast away your ego
to unload the self from darkness
saying farewell to doubts and limbos.
Then come to your heart the tale of Joseph,
the one from Egypt
who left behind his name and fame.
Then come to your tongue the song of the nightingale
the chanting one
who searched for the Eternal rose.

When you ascend to this realm
where the mines rich in spiritual rubies

lighten the trail in thy path
you have reached that uncharted land.
You have found the map of the other world.

The Mountain and the Valley

Listening to nature's echoed words and beholding its posture, we perceive the language of dichotomy. The contrast permeates every aspect of nature.

But it creates wholeness in our surroundings.

The awareness of this most beautiful secret helps us to know about ourselves.

I see the mountains standing tall and visible to all, while the valley below is hidden.

But these two have lived with each other since the beginning of time.

One without the other is incapable of carrying the beauty of perfection.

The extrovert and introvert have become one.

I see the love story between the sun and the moon; one a blazing orb, the giver of light, the other a quiet taker shedding its humble light at night.

The moon wants to be adored only, but the sun stirs life as soon as it appears in the midst of the gathering in nature.

The extrovert and introvert have an everlasting relationship.

I hear the soil's lamentation on the invading roots. The tree's outreaching branches to every direction demands mingling with the most humble and shy giver of all, mother earth.

The extrovert and introvert together provide for all.

As an introvert who was encouraged constantly to be an extrovert, I remember how I used to plea with my parents to leave me out of their social life.

They wanted to take their firstborn to every function they would participate in, trying to do what they were supposed to do, to bring up a balanced kid.

But here is the peculiar part. They would encourage me at the same time to meditate and value my solitude.

I do not know if their effort paid off or not. What I am sure of is that I have not changed much.

I love my solitude.

Then what are these social activities which I have in my house every week?

One for meaningful conversation. One for progress in our intellectual and spiritual life. Another one is to bring a sense of worship and gratitude to our daily lives.

Thus, many of us may claim that we are both introverts and extroverts and, at times, only one.

Regardless of what kind of personality we have and to what category we seem to belong, we all have two aspects in life.

One side of us must seek time to attend to our soul, make time to hear the language of our spirit. To connect with the Divine and to bring spiritual forces home; to our hearts. This solitude is indeed more fruitful than any socializing.

We may look at it as the foundation of human life.

Without it, we might find a void in our life. This universal tone, this ageless need for the human soul, exists in every culture and civilization.

And the other side of us must find a human connection. Celebrating life has to merge with honoring the lives of others. We might say this second aspect reflects reciprocity, the act of receiving and contributing. Even the most extroverted people have to find time to meditate and reflect on the meaning of life.

I live with one of them, my husband, whose extroversion equals itself with his introversion.

Then, words such as ambivert, meaning being someone whose overall behavior is between introversion and extroversion, come to mind.

The finale becomes the different shades of individuality that form the makeup of a colorful garden of humanity.

Meanwhile, immersed in figuring what kind of personality we have or should have or could have had, it comes to the intrusion of the coronavirus in our lives. That uninvited virus crosses the oceans and, without a visa, enters our land and homes, roaming and residing rent-free in the temple of our being. With it comes counting the dead.

Heart broke and saddened, we all witness scenes which we never have eye-witnessed before.

By living, we become the writers of a new chapter in the history of humankind.

We live and grieve by losing lives, watch the dark dust of death passe us.

Isolation and staying home become a new norm.

Is God smiling on some?

Those introverts who now bask in the legitimacy of isolation?

Their lack of sociability goes underground. After all, it is the law of the land that enforces introversion. Even eye contact manifests itself as extroversion.

A paradise for some.

But how about the extroverts?

Their sufferings during the locked-down time entail pain, disappointment, and not knowing what to do with their time at hand.

An opportune moment for the introverts for once to shine through, to provide advice to the opponents. Advice on how to spend the day and how to cope with loneliness. The collective discourse evolves on the benefits of solitude, walking, and reflection on life when you are by yourself!

The ancient craft of attention to the inner life.

This alien-like suggestion baffles many extroverts at first.

But with passing time, most of us search for our inner self.

We learn to absorb the morning breeze.

Silence does not bring discomfort anymore.

Essential questions in life become prominent, and the journey within begins.

We walk in nature and in isolation.

Thus, we observe the existence of the vibrant life outside ourselves. We develop faculty to hear nature's song, the most euphonious melody vouchsafed to all.

On one of the days of the mandatory stay-home, I received a call from a dear friend who is quintessential of an extrovert.

'There are certainly fewer distractions these days,' I hear my friend says on the phone.

She has a busy life. She is always in the state of doing. Her mode of operation is not a daily calendar but an hourly one instead. Never seem to have time for pausing. What I mean is she never reflects. Life is all about traveling, visiting places, and participating in events.

That is it. Her life is eventful.

Our pre-pandemic coffee shop visits were always a rest from her busy schedule and an event for me. With that difference between us, we still enjoy each other's company. So when during the social isolation, on the phone, she says there are fewer distractions in life these days, I am not sure if this is a positive statement or a negative one.

And I wonder how does she live her life with being less busy?

Admittedly, she is a storyteller. Her visits and calls entail a long conversation, on her side, of course. She allows me to express my thought by saying yes or no.

And that is the limit of my participatory role in our conversation.

That is good enough for me.

Her stories are colorful. One is about her eventful trip by train, only to take a photograph of that river in the heart of that mountain.

The other one is, on traveling miles to taste the creation of such and such a chef, or better yet, going out of her way to attend a concert in London only to realize she has arrived two days late.

Then it comes with her accidental invitation to visit the Palace, the Queen, and the late Prince Phillips. She has stories to tell, amazing and amusing at the same time.

"What am I going to do?

They have canceled everything. It is as if they canceled my life," she continues.

Her voice sounds lonely. She has confronted unoccupied time for the first time in her life. Her calendar shows the days of the week with no events imposed on them. This new norm is strange to her.

Maybe even scary.

'What does it mean?' She says.

'How can anybody live like this?

When this thing goes away?'

These questions pollute her sentences. Her disquiet mind analyzes the pain of separation in her life; disconnection from the events, to be precise.

"What are you doing these days?" Is she addressing me?

Is she giving me a chance to talk?

She says: 'I want to know how do you deal with this ordeal?'

How could she be interested in my boring life?

So I prepare myself to answer and seize the chance to have the talking stick in hand for the first time. But it is too late as I hear her answering her own questions too.

'Probably, reading books and writing?' She says.

Wow! What can I say? Back to muteness, I mean listening.

While she catches her breath, I venture to say that it is not a bad idea to embark on reading at this time.

Dismissively and with boredom, she says: 'You know I am not a reader.'

My repressed genius gene pops up, and I hear myself saying: Then, maybe you can write about your adventurous and eventful life. Then, I wait for another dismissive answer.

But, suddenly, as if the sky has cleft asunder, I hear her saying, 'what a divine idea? I can write my memoir!'

She is so excited about this project that she cannot stop talking about it. As if she has never heard about writing.

This writing is like a journey inside, she says. She likes journeying, all right!

Now, she is talkative about writing.

'How should I start?

What part of my life should come first?

Should I write in the morning or evening?'

Questions which she answers herself without any help from me. She is back to normal self.

Living with my husband, a confirmed extrovert, and having friends in that category, has convinced me that there is an invisible bond between these two contrasts in society.

It is the tale of nature manifesting itself in human relationships.

As long as the extrovert and introvert reflect upon their spiritual life, they easily could connect. Therefore, the claim of opposites attracting each other might be well-grounded.

Appeared on reedsy.com

The Pure One

I love biographies, especially when it is about women. The discovery of this love happened when I was a young teenager.

I was raised in a family of readers and note-takers. My father had many books.

Equally, he had many notebooks filled with the notes from the books of poetry and prose that he had read. These notes were precious to him. Indeed he had memorized many of these quotes.

He was a good speaker, and often, he would use the poetry and the thoughts of the Greats, which he had memorized.

Also, he was a prolific letter writer. His letters were poetic prose and long, and that was the extent of his writings. But he never considered himself a writer.

The power of orating and speech was more important to him than writing.

Thus, I do not remember that we ever had any journal in our home. I was never encouraged to write about our trips or our adventures outside.

We had 'notebooks.'

We were encouraged to take notes of the books we read.

Then it came to the telephone. This device did not exist at the time of my parents. In my time, most middle-class families had one in their house.

I discovered soon that instead of letter writing, I could talk with my friends for hours over the phone. We could talk about everything and nothing. Those long conversations with no apparent benefits had one good thing in the store. And that was satisfaction and instant gratification, which letter writing did not have for young people.

That pretty much wrapped up my literary adventure in writing at junior high.

Those are the years which the love of writing in a journal reading literature forms and takes a higher shape. But I was busy chattering over the phone.

One summer night, my family had an invitation to a social gathering.

My parents had to separate me from the phone first which I was glued to, and gently coerce me to go with them.

Reluctantly I consented. The next phone update with my friends about all the girls in our school was in two hours. So it worked for me, and my parents felt triumphant at the same time.

The August breeze had cooled the night. Tall trees, fountains, shrubs, and rows of flowers had made the garden exquisite. Many people were there. Refreshments were on the tables, and servers would pass the trays of sweets. The beautiful house belonged to a philanthropist who had invited people of thought and goodwill.

I was too young to understand if it was fundraising or it was an appreciation ceremony.

Whatever it was, I felt comfortable in being left alone.

People were standing around and talking, and some were sitting and eating. Some were walking around.

Nobody bothered me. I told my parents that I like to go for a walk in the garden.

I had promised myself not to have any sweets until the last, and the most stubborn pimple on my forehead goes away. But the pastries were too good to relinquish them. Pimple or not, I had my plate full of goodies and strolled away.

Each side of the garden had different fountains and statues.

I loved the marble statues of goddess Aurora in the middle of one of the fountains surrounded by Spanish lavender, marigold, and other wildflowers, which I do not remember now.

The water droplets dancing in the air by the gentle wind dampened my skin.

At the end of the garden, there was a brick cottage.

The lights were one and the door open. A welcoming sign with arcing shape of the plaque with a songbird above it said: 'Books for the Friends of Writers.'

I entered the one-room library.

The walls up to top had shelves and were filled with books.

A couple on the other side of the room were reading or browsing the books quietly.

Leather chairs, small tables were situated separately and far from each other.

I remember paintings and tall vases in that house library. For sure, it was not a public one.

I ventured toward the biographies and stories of women. I remember there were books about Helen Keller, Joan of Arc.

I had read them.

It was encouraging. So there are books here that I love, I thought to myself. I put the plate down on one of the tables and browsed more.

Then my eyes fell on a small book which called me to pick it up.

It was at the lowest shelf close to the magazines.

The title was different. It said **'Tahirih the Pure One.'**

I had heard my father reciting poetry from Tahirih. But this book was written by an American woman named Martha Root.

I did not put down the book.

Everything about that small book intrigued me. A woman writer, writing about another woman who is a writer and a poet. I grabbed it. But how could I check it out?

The couple on the other side spotted my clueless look and dilemma. 'The host offers the guests to have any book for three months,' with a cheerful smile, they said.

A thirteen years old girl with a pimple on her face, a book, and a plate of goodies in hand came out of that cottage library that night destined to fall in love with an unknown woman.

I returned to my parents, who were still conversing with other guests. Out of excitement, I noticed that I had not touched the pastries on my plate yet.

The book even, without reading it, had given me the strength to resist.

And I did resist.

It was the beginning of tapping on a transcendental power.

I could not wait to get home and read the book. I do not know what came over me on that summer-starry night, but I knew that I wanted to read more.

The book evoked a feeling of adventure and search in me.

Was I looking for a new vision in life?

But how could it be?

I had not even started to read the book yet. Oh, but it had that aroma of an untouched and maybe a forgotten book.

Finally, my parents consented to leave the party and my father called a taxi.

There was a phone ring as soon as we reached home. I had forgotten about the phone episode. With the book in my hand, I picked up the phone. The voice on the other side, without verifying who picked it up, as she expected me to be the lord of the phone, started to chatter.

My friend was updating me on the last few hours of gossips in our circle.

After a while, I hung up the phone. But I noticed the book still pressed to my chest. Giving no thought to that, I went to my room and opened the book.

The first line of the book grabbed me, *'To understand the story of Tahirih, one should know something of the Iran of her time.'*

The writer took me to the places step b step where her character lived and eventually was killed. Her writing was refreshing. It was a true story about a forgotten woman. That was the power of the story and the hold of the book on me. The writer had traveled to the country of her heroine.

She visited the house Tahirih lived in and her library.

I could see those places in my mind vividly.

There was a mystery about the life of this woman. There were equally unknown facts that made the story even more intriguing.

I fell to sleep with the book that night and the night after.

Tahirih was an outspoken woman living in mid-nineteen century Iran. Her vast knowledge of philosophy, literature, and theology was considered the greatest threat to the ecclesiastical hierarchy and politician.

She had invaded the world of knowledge and search for truth which was a forbidden sin for a woman. She invited the establishment in religion and politics to open debates which were heresy at her time. She was playing with fire.

During her short and difficult life, she remained a writer of prose and poetry of transcendent nature.

Tahirih was from a wealthy and known family. She could have had a comfortable life of an eighteen-century woman. She could have had the approval of her people. With her astonishing beauty and amazing intelligence, she could have had anything she desired. But a high calling took over her life. She gave up the life of the ordinary and gained an unordinary life.

And this book was about her new life.

A pure and transcendent life which she lived with vigor and love for humanity.

One hundred and twenty years later, I read the fragmented story of her life for the first time in my room.

This was one of the first books that was written about Tahirih. A personage which her culture had tried so hard to deny even her existence.

Now this western writer dared to bring her alive out of the dust of refutation and contradiction. Those few who knew of her had kept the flame of love in their hearts.

They would recite her poetry in gatherings.

After reading that book, I wanted to be Tahirih, to be a poet. I wanted to have the power of persuasion and speech like her. And I wanted to die young as a hero like her.

None of these happened in my life.

But the pimples have disappeared.

I still take copious notes from my favorite books.

And most importantly, I inherited one virtue from my hero, and that is not to be afraid of being ostracized.

Appeared on reedsy.com

The Silent Cry

The cry of victims we heard not,
untold sufferings we perceived not.

Justice failed, tyranny victorious,
blood spilled, oppression became unbearable.

Countless lives in the dark, and silence,
succumbed to being "others."

Time passed, history was written,
no page bore their riddle.

Then, the Clouds of Bounty rained,
the heart of man awakened.

The dark night ended,
Dawn's light shed its rays on earth.

Justice took its wings,
consciousness attired itself.

The voiceless found her voice,
the victim claimed her soul.

Music changed its notes,
love poem changed its words.

The pain of others came close to the heart,
never again, nerve again, "others" and "us."

The Silent Lake

When it comes to writing and developing the craft, comparison lingers in the mind of some beginners.

Then we hear the saying: *'comparison is the thief of joy.'*

What joy? Could it mean the joy of writing and being.

Immersed in these thoughts and having these words in mind, I find myself sitting outside on the balcony facing the water.

The soft breeze of the lake and its distant mist awakens my body to the fresh air of the early morning.

The lake lazes calm that morning, and the weather remains pleasant, unlike the other Novembers.

Thus, I take the pen intending to write about what my eye beholds, the lake.

The sun and the lake peacefully embrace each other.

The stillness of the scene betrays the hidden affair between them.

The glass-like lake with its soft ripples mesmerizes the song of contentment, of stillness.

The fiery orb radiates the sky, and its cascade of light shimmers the lake.

Unasked, unpetitioned, the sun gives away warmth; unbashful, untroubled, the lake receives the sun's gift.

How can the feeble pen capture this vivid energy and cage it into the captivity of dull words?

This, the language of God written on nature, the artwork of master Fashioner portrayed on the onlooker's vista.

Has God ever heard His own magnificent writing or witnessed the breathtaking effect of His show on the bewildered observer?

Then the pen moves on the paper, trying to stream my puzzlement:

Why the silence today?

Why is this reflective temper in nature today?

Not perceiving the quest of the question, much less the answer, I continue to be silent, to be present.

The pen remains on the paper without movement and must have been in awe and paralysis of wonder.

The trees basking in the sun stand still like me to witness this spectacular interaction in nature.

Only the happy seabirds flying over the lake remove the deeply intoxicated beholder from the dramatic opera with their song.

I get another cup of coffee and return to my observation, to my space of being.

I witness this glorious silence, this transcendent serenity, and this epic stillness.

The surgeless lake surrounded by hills with blazing fall-color trees lures the soul into the ecstasy of imagination.

Time passes, and I remove the blanket from my back as the sun rises. Not being successful in writing anything that morning, with or without *comparison*, I only discern the joy of absorbing the beauty surrounding me.

The silence of the lake has ushered my soul into stillness, scattering its anguish, removing its uncertainties, and banishing its sorrows.

And with that, my morning reflection and meditation ends.

Meanwhile, the sunlit lake, with no objection to being left alone under the sun, does not even acknowledge my departure!

The Uncommemorated Death

At the age of five, I heard the sound of death for the first time. The wooden coffin went down, and the sound of dirt pouring on the casket, one spade at a time, stayed with me. At a loss to make sense out of the scene, fear visited me, not tears.

What is this?

Why does my grandfather want to sleep in a dark space underground?

I learned nightmare means scary dream, which came to my lot that night and many nights after.

The falling leave had covered the cemetery ground, and the cold breeze serenaded nature with the song of sorrow. My singing song had many notes of question marks.

Can I ever see my grandfather again?

Will he ever visit and bring me gifts?

We all went to my grandmother's home, leaving my beloved grandfather behind in the cold of the Fall. His room, now a silent reminder of his laughter, of times when I would approach him and jump to receive my gift, stood empty.

Years have passed since that Fall day. The loss of a loved one brings me no fear. Not any more. The grief I have to deal with and the sorrow of separation I have to endure. I mourn and even weep. Then I read Rumi:

"Grief can be the garden of compassion.

If you keep your heart open through everything,

your pain can become the greatest ally in your life's search for love and wisdom."

Hence, I have learned to look at death as a different chapter in the book of life. The separation of the sections only connects them to become part of the same book and makes them part of one. Then, we may look at life as extending itself to this material existence and the spiritual realm.

Turning the page to get to the new chapter entails putting the body in the coffin.

Reading the pages in the next chapter of this book needs a new language, a new paradigm.

The letters of transcendence compose the tongue of spiritual life. When the mortal becomes immortal, the next stage starts.

Here is the thing though, the physical death always makes its mark as a remarkable and unforgettable event in life. The end of this first life evokes sorrow, yet reflection on the next life elicits hope.

But, there is the death of other things that are not eventful or commemorated, and only the soul celebrates those death.

One is the death of the ego, the heavy self that fills us with delusions and disappointments. The self that tells us to be the center of the universe, the illiterate self in the language of unity and justice.

In 1979, just graduated in my field, I was ready to start my prosperous life, trod the path of success, and build my castle. Well, not my chateau precisely, but a four-wall space called home. Pursuing my dream in life and let the world circle according to my planned vision.

Being born and raised in ancient culture, the land, where at one time shined as one of the empires trilogies in the world, rubbing shoulders with the Greeks and Romans had given me ideas. Translation: Pride had nestled in my heart, and ego unfurled its wings over my being.

Nothing could go wrong in my Persian life.

Then came the resurgence of fanaticism. And its imposition on the minorities' rights and infringing on the sacredness of their lives. The wave of persecutions and oppression heaped upon many, and death appeared in every space of life.

What I perceived to be my dream evaporated. Questions similar to those questions while standing at the grave of my grandfather crept into my mind.

Why do they heap dirt on my life?

Why do I have to leave my life behind?

The Fall season when I left Iran reminded me of that fall day when I left my grandfather in the cemetery.

Overwhelmed by this sudden test, I tasted pain. Bitter and harsh was the stink of attacks at nights and pillaging the targeted homes. Relatives and loved ones started to disappear and perish.

Uprooted and wiped out, I found myself landed in another country far from my native one. I heard the officer giving the entry visa asking me, *'Business or pleasure?'* I was baffled and muted.

Neither business nor pleasure had taken me to that country. Indeed I had no business and was not pursuing fun there. His focused and searching eyes tried to read any word coming out of my mouth. But there was none.

The long line of travelers waiting behind me triggered my brain into muttering that it is not for business or …, which was interrupted by the deciding words of the officer informing me that, *'Then it is for pleasure.'*

Thus, I entered the West with pleasure.

With no prospect of success in life as I had planned before, my ego started to have a meltdown.

I became a nondescript person. Dwarfing the ego or its disappearance is a process that endures during the whole life. Its death as per se does not register on time; a non-eventful and quiet affair that does not demand recognition or commemoration.

Unlike the physical death that people remember and commemorate, the exact date of the death of the ego is not evident and never commemorated. Emptying the self of the attachments to the world of name and fame is not memorable. Thus, not knowing exactly when it started but being stripped of my material achievement started me on a long journey to higher self-discovery.

I did not have anything to feed my ego anymore.

At first, I resided in a picturesque village on the coast of Northern Ireland.

The facets of life began to unravel themselves with more speed than ever before.

Pain became medicine to heal the wounded self.

One day, I got my hand on a book called **'Paris Talk,'** by Abdu'l-Baha, which helped me make sense of my existence. Probably the most salient question in life has been answered in this book. And that was my question at the time.

When I reached this part, *'**The more the ground is ploughed, the better the seed will grow, the better the harvest will be...,**'* I grasped what I am going through.

It is the suffering that shooing away my ego little by little.

The killing of loved ones and the loss of material wealth of my family back in my country brought sufferings that plowed the field of my spiritual growth.

Detachment, that newborn child of the adversities, arrived.

Then, with the disappearance of attachment, the weight of self became lighter. I did not need all my prideful heritage and achievements to be prosperous.

I learned the alphabet of a new language. The language that celebrates life at any given moment.

Happy the leaf not aware of autumn.

The deer, not seeing its hunter.

Heedless of their pending end.

What pleases them this moment, this day.

The pain and anxiety of being disconnected from the past and not knowing where to turn were too much. I took long walks on the shore of the sea and found awakened moments of bliss. The moments when forgiveness arrives, even forgiving your tormentor, an epilogue to the death of the ego.

I still can see my grandfather's face beaming with joy whenever he visited us. I realize that in his short life, he lived to his reality. Trying to be selfless and filled with the spirit of love, no matter how many times sufferings visited him, he remained joyful and lively.

His life had a deeper bond to the world of existence.

He had a spiritual life which translated itself into the death of the ego.

I can only imagine that his soul happy and dwelling in the celestial realm no matter how many shovels of dirt heaped upon his wooden cover in the grave.

Thus, I try to use whatever meager capacity I have to serve and not to accumulate.

After all, is not this the purpose of every created thing in this world?

The concept of reciprocity?

I try to check that ever-present ego of mine daily and to bring myself to account each day. This journey does not have an end, and that is the beauty of life.

* Maternal grandfather

Appeared on medium.com in 2021

Where is Home?

A happy childhood makes you long to go back to that time and space. And that is the case with me.

If it was not for my early years of a carefree childhood, I might not have withstood life's unexpected and turbulent episodes.

My parents' house had a yard with a flower garden, trees, and butterflies.

I see myself at four chasing life in that yard. I see myself leaving the world of the adults behind to submerge myself in nature's offerings.

Every day with different gifts. One day drops of rain, another wind, and sunshine.

But they were all mine.

It was my made-up world in which nature had given me ownership.

We used to have breakfast outside during the summertime. Under the shade of the trees, the singing birds were our morning companions. The jasmine bushes with their intoxicating aroma wafting through the bedroom window were my call to wake up reluctantly.

'How is my poet's jasmine this morning?' I would hear Mom admiring her flowers.

Then she would turn to her lilacs and roses.

The conversation would go on between these two species in creation very well.

Who says we can't talk to our other peers? Plants and animals?

For one, my mother knew the language very well.

The alphabet of the inter-species language is love, and she knew that well.

I believe she could even hear them as well too. Otherwise, why would she do this every day?

I do not know why the 'poet' dragged into the name of the flower jasmine. But certainly, I can guess. They have the most intense fragrance, and the whole summer, they are in bloom.

So, it is possible that anybody with the power of reflection, charmed by this perfumed flower, would put down a word or two in an intoxicating mood. Voila!

Here comes the reason for the abundance of poetry in the East.

Who can resist writing when facing inspiring emotions surging within?

And the ever-present ambiance of an abundance of perfumed flowers, nightingales, butterflies, and shaded tall trees would vibrate the deepest refined sentiments in any human being, fertile ground to breed poetry.

After breakfast, I was on my own. My world was in that yard. In mid-morning, Mom would call me to go in to have my fruits. Then, again I was free, back to playing with sticks, chasing butterflies, climbing trees, picking up apples, and follow the trail of ants.

Every day was a new day.

When we are at a tender age, we never get tired of watching and following ants to their hole.

Learning is through visual, hearing, touching, and tasting. Digesting our surroundings is through the experiential approach.

And that is why they are endlessly exciting to us. We live the words of Emily Dickinson.

The Child's faith is new –
Whole – like His Principle –
Wide – like the Sunrise
On fresh Eyes –
Never had a Doubt

The call for the launch was a break to my hands and clothing, stained with raspberries and dirt. The routine of washing hands, changing clothing, and eating had to be followed by me.

For as long as I remember, I spent the long days of summer in that yard.

Those days are so long ago, so far away, and yet so near and more vivid than ever.

It is one of the mysteries of the age. You get closer to your childhood. And the chapters in between dwarf.

You dwell in that first chapter of your life and that space more and more. Why?

Now we hear that our early childhood experiences shape our adult life: that people with positive experiences in childhood are associated with lower rates of depression.

If that is true, then everyone has to have a happy childhood.

What can we do about that?

How can we help to bring about this given right of the youngsters?

The childhood backyard with carefree joy and happiness should be in everyone's book of life.

Back to my happy yard, for many fortunate ones, it is possible not only to travel in time and reminisce on their childhood but even to trace the physical place that provided their happy memories.

I am not one of them.

I never can go back to the home where I grew up. I am forbidden. I cannot return home ever.

Oh, yes, I had a happy childhood. I grew up to my twenties, and my good life continued.

Then, a sudden change trembled my world with an unforeseeable speed.

It was 1979 when quiet days of life transformed into days with deep anxiety and uncertainty.

I had to leave the happy yard behind, the one which by now had transformed into a mature yard with new attractions.

On a cloudy day in September, with one suitcase in hand, I left my life behind.

The last thing I remember before I left the birth land is my parents' worried eyes. As if they were watching their firstborn heading to embrace a deep fall and having no ability to help.

I waved goodbye to them after a long hug.

Then, I crept into the plane.

In an emotional daze and numbness, I sat there immersed in the ocean of grief. I looked outside to find my parents' faces against all odds. Maybe they were able to persuade the guards to let them pass the red line. And like the movies, they could appear at the end of the plane magically.

With my eyes walking the land, I watched the plane take off to the sky of Iran.

With closing my eyes, I tried to have my parents near me.

An announcement came that we can release ourselves from the belt buckles. I looked out the window feeling the tears on my face.

I saw clouds in vapor shape drifting freely against the blue color of the sky. It took me another time another place, seeing myself looking up through the tall trees and see the white clouds moving over my head.

By the time stewardess served the coffee, I find myself writing down these words in a small notebook: 'I take my clouds with me.' After all, they were my clouds as were everyone else's cloud.

The 'takers' could not take that away from me.

Can I ever go back to my land?

The question lingered for the whole trip. Can I ever?

What will be my destiny in an unknown space?

Focus on the present time, I told myself.

Start writing about now. It is the best way to distract yourself from the blow of sudden uprooting.

My hands went over the silk scarf around my neck. Mom gave this at the last minute at the Airport. Yes, I should write about things which distant me from the big elephant in the room, 'My uprooting.' Thus, on the next page, after my claim on the cloud, I wrote, Mom, you are with me always.

I do not remember what I wrote next.

With no appetite to eat anything, I was drinking coffee during the whole flight.

Somehow the coffee's effect on that day was magical. It kept me dry of tears. It worked, and I have no scientific proof backing this theory.

Hours later, I landed in Germany. By the time I left the Airport, it was dark.

I looked up and saw stars shinning with the same luminosity as in my land. Oh, how great this is. I have my stars here too! A moment of bliss arrived.

But it vanished as quickly as it had appeared. The thought of what I am going to do now took over my being.

And that was the beginning of my intercontinental living.

Many years have passed since that flight which took me away from my birth home. And many times, I have traversed the oceans and mountains in my mind to reach my childhood home.

But I can never step in that house in the world of matter.

That house has been possessed unlawfully by others who claimed everything else in my life.

Backed by the Islamic government, strangers pillaged, illegally possessed, killed, and disowned the rightful owners.

In the case of my parents, they imprisoned them and disowned them.

What right do I have now to the home of my childhood?

They claimed it and registered it in the books of their laws.

Thus, they closed the door of my return to my homeland.

Reflecting on my childhood memory has sustained me during all these years of finding my way ahead. Whatever that path has been, I always remember the clouds, ants, and butterflies, but mostly the poet jasmine in our yard, a place where I am forbidden to step in.

I solace myself with these words of Thomas Hood:

I remember, I remember,

The house where I was born,

The little window where the sun

Came peeping in at morn,

If the home is where we are, then mine has been all over.

The journey continues.

But what is most dear to us is unpossessable by the strangers.

And in my case, they could not possess or pillage my memories.

Appeared on reedsy.com